Alphabet Books

An Alphabet Salad

Fruits and Vegetables from A to Z

by Sarah L. Schuette

Consultant:
Joan Bushman, MPH, RD
American Dietetic Association

Capstone
press

Mankato, Minnesota

A is for apple.

Apples have smooth skin.
Their skin can be red, yellow,
or green. Apples crunch
when eaten.

B is for banana.

Bananas grow in bunches called hands.

Each banana in the hand is a finger.

Aa Bb Cc Dd Ee Ff Gg Hh Ii Jj Kk Ll Mm Nn Oo Pp Qq Rr Ss Tt Uu Vv Ww Xx Yy Zz

C is for carrot.

Carrots are long roots that people

eat. Most carrots are orange.

Others are red or purple.

Aa Bb Cc Dd Ee Ff Gg Hh Ii Jj Kk Ll Mm Nn Oo Pp Qq Rr Ss Tt Uu Vv Ww Xx Yy Zz

D is for date.

Dates have shiny skin. Ripe dates
are fat, but their skin is wrinkled.

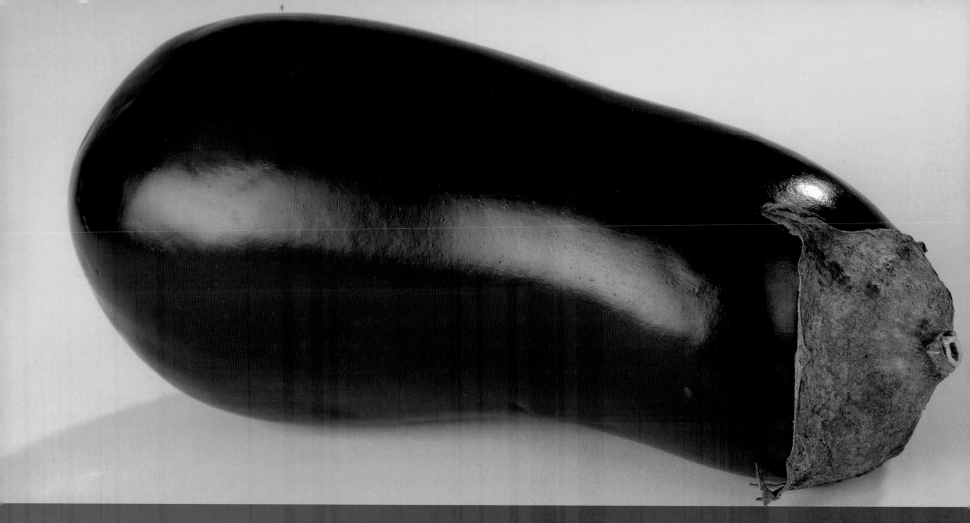

E is for eggplant.

Eggplant tastes best when cooked.

An eggplant is a purple vegetable.

Aa Bb Cc Dd Ee Ff Gg Hh Ii Jj Kk Ll Mm Nn Oo Pp Qq Rr Ss Tt Uu Vv Ww Xx Yy Zz

F is for fig.

Figs are soft fruits that taste sweet. The sugar in figs gives people energy.

G is for grape.

Grapes grow on a vine
in bunches. They have
smooth skin.

H is for honeydew melon.

Honeydew melons got their name because they are sweet and juicy. They are good in salads and desserts.

9

I is for Italian parsley.

Italian parsley is an herb.
Parsley adds flavor to foods
that do not have much taste.

10

J is for jackfruit.

Jackfruit tastes a little like a banana. It is the world's largest fruit that grows on trees. One jackfruit can equal the weight of four watermelons.

K is for kiwifruit.

Kiwifruit are fuzzy and brown
on the outside. The fruit inside
a kiwi is green and juicy.

L is for lemon.

Lemons have yellow outsides. Juice from a lemon adds flavor to salads and other foods.

M is for mushroom.

Mushrooms look like small umbrellas.

The top of a mushroom is called a cap.

Aa Bb Cc Dd Ee Ff Gg Hh Ii Jj Kk Ll **Mm** Nn Oo Pp Qq Rr Ss Tt Uu Vv Ww Xx Yy Zz

N is for nectarine.

Nectarines have pits. Each pit holds a seed that can grow into a tree.

O is for onion.

Onions smell strong. Sometimes the smell makes a person's eyes water.

Aa Bb Cc Dd Ee Ff Gg Hh Ii Jj Kk Ll Mm Nn Oo Pp Qq Rr Ss Tt Uu Vv Ww Xx Yy Zz

P is for pineapple.

Pineapples look like pinecones. But a pineapple has sweet, yellow fruit inside its hard shell.

Q is for quince.

Quinces taste like apples
and pears put together.
Most people cook these
fruits before eating them.

18

R is for radish.

Radishes grow underground.
They can be red, white, or
black. Radishes have a
peppery taste.

S is for strawberry.

Strawberries are the only fruit with seeds on the outside. One strawberry might have 200 seeds.

T is for tomato.

Tomatoes are the world's most popular fruit. Tomatoes are used in ketchup, spaghetti sauce, pizza, and many other foods.

21

U is for uglifruit.

Uglifruit tastes a little like a grapefruit.

The uglifruit's peel is bumpy.

V is for navel orange.

The navel orange has a bellybutton. Sweet fruit grows in sections inside the orange.

W is for watermelon.

People can tap on the outside of a watermelon. A hollow sound means it is ready to eat.

X is for wax bean.

Wax beans have yellow pods. They are a cousin of the green bean, but they have a waxier shine.

Y is for yam.

The yam is often called a sweet potato. At Thanksgiving, people cook yams with brown sugar and marshmallows to make candied yams.

Z is for zucchini.

Zucchini is a member of the squash family. People make zucchini breads, pickles, cakes, and stews.

Fruit and Vegetable Facts

Apple
- has seeds inside the skin
- floats in water

Banana
- becomes ripe after picking
- turns from green to yellow when ripe

Carrot
- is a root vegetable
- has beta-carotene for healthy eyes

Date
- has a large seed in the middle
- grows in clusters

Eggplant
- grows well in warm weather
- covered with thin skin on the outside

Fig
- needs to grow in places where it is hot
- can be yellow, pink, green, or brown

Grape
- often has seeds
- turns into a raisin when dried

Honeydew melon
- grows on a vine
- belongs to the gourd family

Italian parsley
- often used as a decoration
- can be picked and used right away

Jackfruit
- can weigh 40 pounds (18 kilograms)
- first grown in India

Kiwifruit
- sweetens at room temperature
- grows to be the size of an egg

Lemon
- is a citrus fruit
- grows on a tree

Mushroom
- used as medicine in some countries
- has more than 2,500 varieties

Nectarine
- ripens off the tree
- related to roses

Onion
- grows underground as a bulb
- eaten raw or cooked

Pineapple
- grows on the ground
- topped with crown of leaves

Quince
- has seeds inside
- makes tasty jelly

Radish
- is a root vegetable
- grows well in cool weather

Strawberry
- usually picked by hand
- has green, leafy tops

Tomato
- sometimes called "love apples"
- rich in vitamins A and C

Uglifruit
- cross of a tangerine and a grapefruit
- native to the island of Jamaica

Navel orange
- makes juice
- smells sweet when ripe

Watermelon
- has white and black seeds inside
- made mostly of water

Wax bean
- sometimes called "butter beans"
- can be eaten raw or cooked

Yam
- is a stem vegetable
- can weigh as much as 100 pounds (45 kilograms)

Zucchini
- means "little squashes" in Italian
- is usually green

Fats, Oils and Sweets

Dairy Group
2-3 servings

Protein Group
2-3 servings

Vegetable Group 3-5 servings

Fruit Group 2-4 servings

Grain Group 6-11 servings

**Use the Food Guide Pyramid
to see how many servings you should eat every day.**

Words to Know

ripe—ready to be eaten or picked; foods may change color or shape when they are ripe.

root—the part of a plant or tree that grows underground; some roots can be eaten as vegetables.

seed—the part of a plant that can grow into a new plant

vine—a plant with a long stem that grows along the ground; vines can also grow up fences, buildings, or other places.

Read More

Barron, Rex. *Fed Up! A Feast of Frazzled Foods.* New York: Putnam, 2000.

Nelson, Robin. *Vegetables.* First Step Nonfiction. Minneapolis: Lerner Publications, 2003.

Richards, Jean. *A Fruit Is a Suitcase for Seeds.* Brookfield, Conn.: Millbrook Press, 2002.

Rondeau, Amanda. *Fruits Are Fun.* What Should I Eat? Edina, Minn.: Abdo Publishing, 2002.

Internet Sites

Track down many sites about fruits and vegetables. Visit the FACT HOUND at *http://www.facthound.com*

IT IS EASY! IT IS FUN!

1) Go to *http://www.facthound.com*

2) Type in: 0736816836

3) Click on "FETCH IT" and FACT HOUND will find several links hand-picked by our editors.

Relax and let our pal FACT HOUND do the research for you!

Index

A+ Books are published by Capstone Press
P.O. Box 669, 151 Good Counsel Drive, Mankato, Minnesota 56002
http://www.capstone-press.com

1 2 3 4 5 6 08 07 06 05 04 03

Library of Congress Cataloging-in-Publication Data
Schuette, Sarah L., 1976–
    An alphabet salad: fruits and vegetables from A to Z / by Sarah L. Schuette.
        p.cm.—(Alphabet Books)
    Summary: Introduces fruits and vegetables through photographs and brief text that describe one item for each letter of the alphabet.
    Includes bibliographical references and index.
    ISBN 0-7368-1683-6 (hardcover)
    1. Fruit—Juvenile literature. 2. Vegetables—Juvenile literature. 3. Salads—Juvenile literature. 4. English language—Alphabet—Juvenile literature. [1. Fruit. 2. Vegetables. 3. Alphabet.] I. Title. II. Series: Alphabet Books (Mankato, Minn.)
SB357.2 .S38 2003
634—dc21   2002015066

Credits
Heather Kindseth, designer; Gary Sundermeyer, photographer; Keith Karasic Photography, 11; PhotoDisc, Inc., 1, 30

Note to Parents, Teachers, and Librarians

An Alphabet Salad uses color photographs and a nonfiction format to introduce children to various fruits and vegetables while building mastery of the alphabet. It is designed to be read aloud to a pre-reader or to be read independently by an early reader. The images help early readers and listeners understand the text and concepts discussed. The book encourages further learning by including the following sections: Fruit and Vegetable Facts, Words to Know, Read More, Internet Sites, and Index. Early readers may need assistance using these features.

DATE DUE
